INTRODUCTION

All praise due to The Supreme Intellect of the Universe, YHWH, for giving me the inspiration to bring His Truth. I have decided to write a collection of small, insightful reads for my people; easy to read scrolls that get straight to the point. These works will keep the reader's attention using images and language breakdowns.

This first writing will survey the deeper mysteries of Noah from the initiate's perspective. Most of these deeper truths that I am bringing to light are the product of intense study. The rest of these truths are the product of intuition or Divine Revelation. I encourage those who will collect these scrolls to pass them down to their children, so that their offspring will be greatly rooted in Torah. My work here is to arm YAH's soldiers In the physical and spiritual warfare of our present existence.

My birth name is Yashuv-EL. Its numerical value according to Gematria is 349; it is a blend of energies of 3, 4 and 9. The number 3 resonates with joy, compassion, encouragement, and talent. It also reflects abundance, or the increase that is the result of a broad thinking process. This number is powerful because it also means that I'm surrounded by Ascending Masters. Behind the veil, they assist me along my journey. They are ancient prophets who ascended to, and teach from, the spirit realm. This can be supported from scripture:

כג הִנֵּה אָנֹכִי שֹׁלֵחַ לָכֶם, אֵת אֵלִיָּה הַנָּבִיא--לִפְנֵי, בּוֹא יוֹם יְהוָה, הַגָּדוֹל, וְהַנּוֹרָא. כד וְהֵשִׁיב לֵב-אָבוֹת עַל-בָּנִים, וְלֵב בָּנִים עַל-אֲבוֹתָם--

Malachi 4:5-6/3:23-24 "Behold, I will send you Elijah the prophet before the coming of the great and dreadful day of the Lord: And he shall turn the hearts of the father to the children, and the hearts of the children back to their fathers--"

This verse is written after Elijah, the prophet, "ASCENDED". The number 4 is a sign of will, devotion, passion and drive. 9 is the manifestation of consciousness, signifying that I am a light bearer and a humanitarian.

REMOVING THE VEIL

Many of the ancient writings speak to the masses, but veil their secrets behind allegorical symbolism. Remember the saying, "If you want to hide it from a black person put it in a book"? I truly don't believe this statement is meant to say that black people don't read, rather it is saying that we, as black people, only look at these things from a physical perspective. We don't see the spiritual message that is there for us to internalize.

To prove my point let us look at 2 movies: one is *Jack and the Beanstalk*, and the other is *American Tail*. If I was to ask you what the first one was about you would probably say that "it's about a man who sold his cow for a magical bean. The bean grew into a stalk that rose to the heavens where there was gold and giants--who Jack triumphed over." When asked about the latter, you would most likely go on to mention that the plot involves a mouse, which, moved from Europe to America to escape the cats, but realized that there are cats in America also. Both responses are correct, yet do not capture the true message the writer was trying to convey. *Jack and the Beanstalk* have everything to do with meditation. The cow, Milky White, is the white phase in meditation. The seed represents the dormant energy at the base of the spine. The beanstalk symbolizes the spine and Kundalini energy rising. In Alchemy, gold represents the highest level of consciousness. The giants--who must be destroyed-- represent our EGO.

Let us look at American *Tail* a little more in depth, and further remove the curtains that the oppressors have put over our eyes. This movie is truly speaking of the persecutions that the Jews were experiencing in Germany at the hands of the Nazis--who are represented by cats. The families of the mice were the Jews that fled to America--where they believed there weren't any cats (racists). Come to find out that they couldn't have been more wrong.

The Torah is no different; it is broken down into four different levels; the Peshat, which is the simple interpretation; the Remez level, which means hint in Hebrew; the Drash, a regal level; and the Sod, which is the Secret level. We will cover a lot of ground in this short reading.

ר"ש אמר ווי להההוא ב"נ דאמר דהא אורייתא אתא לאחזאה ספורין בעלמא ומלין דהדיוטי. דאי הכי אפילו בזמנא דא אנן יכלין למעבד אורייתא במלין דהדיוטי ובשבחא יתיר מכלהו אי לאחזאה מלה דעלמא אפילו אינון קפסירי דעלמא אית ביינייהו מלין עלאין יתיר. אי הכי נזיל אבתרייהו ונעביד מנייהו אורייתא כהאי גוונא אלא כל מלין דאורייתא מלין עלאין אינון ורזין עלאין

Rabbi Simeon says: "Woe to the man who says that the Torah came to relate stories, simply and plainly, [and simpleton talks about Esau and Laban and the like]. If it was so, even at the present day we could produce a Torah from simplistic matters, and perhaps even nicer ones than those. If the Torah came to exemplify worldly matters, even the rulers of the world have among them things that are superior. If so, let us follow them and produce from them a Torah in the same manner. It must be that all items in the Torah are of a superior nature and are uppermost secrets

(Zohar, parashatBahalotekha)

Here is a quote by mister Zohar himself:

"Those who attack the Scriptures usually approach the scriptures from a simplistic angle. Their ignorance blocks them from transcending and receiving the greater message, as well as the keys of enlightenment. Throughout history, there has never been a book written that was greater than the Torah. The Torah covers every area of learning in life; Physics, Metaphysics, History, Mathematics, Psychology, and Physiology." You name it, our Sages knew it.

"Moses, our master, physiologized"

–Joesephus-

CAIN AND ABEL AND THE HUMAN PSYCHE

Right before the ParashatNoakh (portion of Noah), the stage is set by describing the polarity of the human psyche. This is illustrated in the lesson of Cain and Abel. Keep in mind though, there are many other deep interpretations of this story. For instance, we see an entirely different exegesis in an article by Ruben:

"…. so the story of Cain and Abel may be interpreted in different ways. For sure, jealousy between brothers is still raging through the human psyche… and it may simply be that and its consequences.

But today I read that it may be the story of how the Neanderthal man, Abel -who would have hunted for flesh-- was killed off by homosapiens--who developed methods of growing grain… which enabled humans to settle, build villages, and to eventually develop civilization--ranging from handwriting and numbers to laws and taxation and of course, war. Ironically, the home of civilization is the Middle East. So Cain and Abel were from different species, but both human and the story may be about guilt; that we killed other humans and remain aggressive and warlike."

Note that Ruben's understanding of the story, as it relates to jealousy, comes from the relationship between the Hebrew word for the name Cain (קין/Qayin) and the Hebrew word meaning jealousy (קנא/Qanna'). Both of these stem from the Hebrew root קנא/q-n-a. This is why Ruben starts off by saying that Cain and Abel is a story about jealousy. The root קנא is also very interesting because not only is it attached to the idea of jealousy, but it is also connected to the idea of acquisition, in the context of acquiring riches, or possessions. This is why Gabriel haTalmid interprets it the following way, which is entirely different from the above interpretation:

> The story of Cain and Abel is an allegorization of the inherent conflict between the nomadic pastoralist culture-from which the Israelite culture emerged- and the agriculturalist culture, which gave rise to the first nation states, such as Egypt. These two forms of food production are what followed the food collecting stage which is alluded to in the Garden of Eden story. The idea of the food production stage supersedes the food collecting stage in human history is even alluded to in the story of Ham, Shem, and Japeth, who do not necessarily refer to people, but rather are tied to the rise of the very first global centers of food production which appeared during the early Holocene epoch. These are found in South Eastern Sahara(Ham); in the plateau area of the middle east which stretches from Palestine and Syria through southern Turkey and Iran(Shem); and in the tropical rainforest zone of southern East Asia(Japeth).
>
> With the production of food (as opposed to the collection of food/Edenic period of humanity) came conditions that would lay the foundation needed for the first nation states. This is alluded to in the Tanakh when it describes Cain/Qayin building a city (B'reishith/Genesis 4:17). Along with the emergence of these first nation states, we also see, in some cases the emergence of social stratification and groups of people who amassed material wealth. This is all tied to Cain/Qayin's name, which is not only connected to the Hebrew word for jealousy, but also connected to the idea of acquisition (both coming from קנא/q-n-a). Jealousy and acquisition are connected because in many cases, the acquiring of

material possessions, or 'keeping up with the Jones's', is connected to jealousy, and the desire to emulate the people around you, who themselves are emulating those within the upper hierarchies of the state. This mindset, in which one becomes a slave to their possessions, leads to the further subjugation of slavery to the state-- in territory, thinking and cultural values.

The Nomadic Pastoral cultures, on the other hand (represented by Abel as opposed to Cain), having no such ties or allegiance, live on the periphery of the state. This perspective gives them a sense of autonomy which allows them to be critical of not only the state, but also its propensity to perpetuate violence, and greed, at the expense of its subjects. This is why the Egyptians could sell themselves, and their land to Pharaoh (Genesis 47:15-20), while the Israelites and their land can never be sold in perpetuity (Leviticus 25). This conflict of values is what is being communicated in the scriptures. Abel, who symbolized pastoral values (the values of Israel for example, who later developed agricultural practices and states themselves), and whose offering was pleasing to the Creator, was killed by Cain, who represented agriculturalist values which gave rise to the nation state (Egypt being among the first of the nation states). The conflict between pastoralist values and the values of the state are evidenced in the experiences of the Bedouins of the modern Middle East, whose nomadic nature is despised by many states of the region. It is also evidenced in revival of pastoralism in Central Asia after the collapse of the Soviet Union. The Tanakh, which in many ways is a codification of Israelite Pastoral wisdom, further hints to the tension between pastoralist and the state in Bereshith 43:32, and 46:34.

Notice that there are several interpretations to this single story. This is because the Torah was *meant* to be understood in several different ways. Look at Psalms 62:12, which reads --אַחַת, דִּבֶּר אֱלֹהִים שְׁתַּיִם-זוּ שָׁמָעְתִּי, once has God spoken, twice I have heard. How can a person hear twice when God speaks once? This is because the words of the Supreme Intellect of the Universe contain wisdom which is inexhaustible. This idea is alluded to in the Gemara (Sanhedrin 34a), which says of this verse:

> מקרא אחד יוצא לכמה טעמים ואין טעם אחד יוצא מכמה מקראות / One [section of] scripture, [can] emerge [to convey different] meanings, but a single meaning cannot be deduced from several scriptures.

> דבי ר' ישמעאל תנא (ירמיהו כג) וכפטיש יפוצץ סלע מה פטיש זה מתחלק לכמה ניצוצות אף מקרא אחד יוצא לכמה טעמים Of the house of Rabbi Yishmael, it was taught (Jer 23:29) 'As a hammer shattered/opened a stone': Just as a rock [that] is divided into splinters, so can one scripture produce [different] meanings.

This is why it is important to look at several different interpretations of the scripture. From this comes enlightenment. This is why Hebrew Israelites should never allow ourselves to be divided over different allegorical interpretations of the stories in Torah, for it is a book of 70 faces.

As we look deeper into the story of Cain and Abel, we can even see that the story may even have something to say on different points of view. Notice that the word Cain also means spear. We can then, see the idea of pushing our points of view, in terms of the root Cain(קַיִן)/Qayin, meaning to spear or thrust). The essence of Cain comes out of us when we are pushing our own point of view, or when we become defensive when another perspective seems to be infringing on our narrow views. This is due to the fact that we are slaves to our lower self. This 'slavery to self' subjugates you to your carnal instincts. When your views are being attacked, your brain releases norepinephrine, which is the same fluid that releases if you were being physically attacked. When it enters the body, it throws off the limbic system and sends you into a primitive state. This is why people become so aggressive when they debate.

The Ego, when being challenged, doesn't care about being right, it only cares about being dominant and victorious. If we look back, when we are calm, we can identify when Cain entered the conversation. When an egotistical person is crushed, he feels that there is injustice and becomes bent on revenge.

Let us also understand that Cain also operates silently. Even more, Cain will even destroy something it is involved in, proving its point by not giving its best effort.

Now Abel/הֶבֶל in Hebrew means emptiness. Abel represents pure thoughts. People who have a clear mind are at peace and become perfect vessels for the Divine Force. Depression on the other hand, is caused by excessive thinking.

We read in the Book of Genesis/Bereshiyt, in the fourth chapter that jealousy (Cain) kills off pure thoughts (Abel) which causes man to be a wanderer, detached from man and His Maker. This is alluded to in the story when it says of Cain: וַיֵּשֶׁב בְּאֶרֶץ-נוֹד, קִדְמַת-עֵדֶן/ "and he dwelled in the land of Nod (נוֹד), east Eden." Though Nod is the name of a place, its root נוד actually means to wander, or flee.

Envy and jealousy is an offshoot of the spirit of laziness. Laziness leads to corruption, violence and slavery (harsh servitude). The lazy watches the hard worker builds and when the time is right; he will attack and rob the diligent. The lazy will also watch the bright minds that are studious and are innovators. He will then subject them to servitude, to be the brains of their empire. These oppressed intellectuals are forced to use their knowledge for corruption, to benefit the oppressor. So naturally, when the earth is filled with corruption, it goes into a chaotic state and resets itself.

ה וַיַּרְא יְהוָה, כִּי רַבָּה רָעַת הָאָדָם בָּאָרֶץ, וְכָל-יֵצֶר מַחְשְׁבֹת לִבּוֹ, רַק רַע כָּל-הַיּוֹם. ו וַיִּנָּחֶם יְהוָה, כִּי-עָשָׂה אֶת-הָאָדָם בָּאָרֶץ; וַיִּתְעַצֵּב, אֶל-לִבּוֹ. ז וַיֹּאמֶר יְהוָה, אֶמְחֶה אֶת-הָאָדָם אֲשֶׁר-בָּרָאתִי מֵעַל פְּנֵי הָאֲדָמָה, מֵאָדָם עַד-בְּהֵמָה, עַד-רֶמֶשׂ וְעַד-עוֹף הַשָּׁמָיִם: כִּי נִחַמְתִּי, כִּי עֲשִׂיתִם. ח וְנֹחַ, מָצָא חֵן בְּעֵינֵי יְהוָה.

Genesis 6:5-8 "And the LORD saw that the wickedness of man was great in the earth, and that every imagination of the thoughts of his heart was only evil continually **6** *And it repented the LORD that He had made man on the earth, and it grieved Him at His heart* **7** *And the LORD said: 'I will blot out man whom I have created from the face of the earth; both man, and beast, and creeping thing, and fowl of the air; for it repenteth Me that I have made them* **8** *But Noah found grace in the eyes of the LORD."*

Of course these verses, which refer to the almighty repenting (וַיִּנָּחֶם יְהוָה), are anthropomorphisms, being that a Supreme Intellect does not have human characteristics.

לֹא אִישׁ אֵל וִיכַזֵּב, וּבֶן-אָדָם וְיִתְנֶחָם; הַהוּא אָמַר וְלֹא יַעֲשֶׂה, וְדִבֶּר וְלֹא יְקִימֶנָּה.

Numbers 23:19 "God is not a man, that He should lie, Nor a son of man, that He should repent; Has He said, and will He not do it?"

God/Elohiym speaks in the language of man, so men can relate. Anthropomorphism comes from two Greek words:

anthropos/ἄνθρωπος (man) and morphe/μορφή (form). The anthropomorphism in this verse is used to spark grief in the heart of men. It is NOT to show that Elohiym has repented. YHWH means He always was, He always is, and always shall be. This is conveyed by our English word infinite. When the words, Elohym/ אֱלֹהִים or EL /אֵל (which is related to the Greek word Elector/ἠλέκτωρ originates) come to us in English (from the Greek) it gives us the English word, Electric. This relates to energy. 'YHWH Elohym' (יְהוָה אֱלֹהִים) or 'Infinite energy' is beyond human emotion.

DELUGE STORIES

As we enter deeper into this deluge story, we must keep in mind that there are over 500 hundred flood stories in the world. These include the Epic of Gilgamesh, as well as tales told by the Mandaeans of southern Iraq, whose religion was influenced by John the Baptist. The Mandeans also believe the Ark rests in Egypt. Hinduism and Islam also have their own flood stories. So to say one is plagiarized from another would be incorrect. In fact, the claim that the Babylonian flood predates the Bible by thousands of years is absurd. This can be disproven with some brief research.

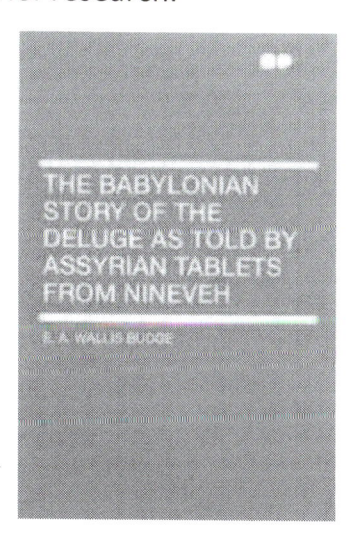

In the book, *The Babylonian Story of the Deluge as told by the Assyrian Tablets from Nineveh*, the author E.A Wallis Budge states that Ashur Bani Pal loves Sumerian writings. It's easy to distinguish between works belonging to the Ashur-Bani-Pal private library, and the works of the temple of Nebo. The short colophon on the tablets of the king's library reads: "palace of Ashur-Bani-Pal, king of host, king of the country of Assyria" & that of the library of Nebo reads "country of Ashur-Bani-Pal, king of host, king of Assyria."

Ok, to make it simple, the copies of the Babylonian deluge story we have reads, "palace of Ashur-Bani-Pal, king of host, king of the country of Assyria." This means this is a rewrite and a revised edition done by Ashur-Bani-Pal who is Esar-Haddon/אֵסַר חַדֹּן of the Bible.

וַיִּשְׁמְעוּ, צָרֵי יְהוּדָה וּבִנְיָמִן : כִּי-בְנֵי הַגּוֹלָה בּוֹנִים הֵיכָל, לַיהוָה אֱלֹהֵי יִשְׂרָאֵל. ב וַיִּגְּשׁוּ אֶל-זְרֻבָּבֶל וְאֶל-רָאשֵׁי הָאָבוֹת, וַיֹּאמְרוּ לָהֶם נִבְנֶה עִמָּכֶם--כִּי כָכֶם, נִדְרוֹשׁ לֵאלֹהֵיכֶם ; וְלֹא (וְלוֹ) אֲנַחְנוּ זֹבְחִים, מִימֵי אֵסַר חַדֹּן מֶלֶךְ אַשּׁוּר, הַמַּעֲלֶה אֹתָנוּ, פֹּה.

Ezra 4:1-2 4 "Now when the adversaries of Judah and Benjamin heard that the descendants of the captivity were building the temple of the Lord God of Israel; ² *Then they came to Zerubbabel and the heads of the fathers' houses, and said to them, Let us build with you, for we seek your God as you do; and we have sacrificed to Him since the days of Esarhaddon king of Assyria, who brought us here."*

We see here that Ezra is speaking with individuals who claim that Esar-Haddon/אֵסַר חַדֹּן, also known as Ashur-Bani-Pal, brought them to that particular place. This is happened during approximately 600 BC. Hence, we have proven that the Hebrew story of the deluge predated Esar Haddon's story. Let us continue now that that is settled.

Right before the Flood, the Creator said that He would reduce mankind's lifespan.

וַיֹּאמֶר יְהוָה, לֹא-יָדוֹן רוּחִי בָאָדָם לְעֹלָם, בְּשַׁגַּם, הוּא בָשָׂר ; וְהָיוּ יָמָיו, מֵאָה וְעֶשְׂרִים שָׁנָה
Genesis 6:3 And the Lord said, my spirit shall not always strive with man, [in his error] for that he also is flesh: yet his days shall be an hundred and twenty years.

This drastic reduction of life from around 900 years to 120 can be explained by what is called the Canopy theory. The earth's atmosphere is known to have six layers. According to the Canopy theory, the earth also has a seventh layer. This seventh layer is created from ice, which has been suspended in the magnetic field. This layer of ice would block out UV lights and increase air pressure. Today, the seventh layer is a 100 miles thick. In the time of Parashat Noakh, the thickness was doubled. The resulting increase of Earth's air pressure would turn the planet into a giant greenhouse, causing things to grow in excess. We find evidence which supports the Canopy theory even in the Tanakh:

וַיַּעַשׂ אֱלֹהִים, אֶת-הָרָקִיעַ, וַיַּבְדֵּל בֵּין הַמַּיִם אֲשֶׁר מִתַּחַת לָרָקִיעַ, וּבֵין הַמַּיִם אֲשֶׁר מֵעַל לָרָקִיעַ; וַיְהִי-כֵן

Genesis 1:7 And God made the firmament, and divided the waters which were under the firmament from the waters which were above the firmament; and it was so.

הַלְלוּ-יָהּ:
א.הַלְלוּ אֶת-יְהוָה, מִן-הַשָּׁמַיִם;   הַלְלוּהוּ, בַּמְּרוֹמִים.
ב.הַלְלוּהוּ כָל-מַלְאָכָיו;   הַלְלוּהוּ, כָּל-צְבָאָו.
ג.הַלְלוּהוּ, שֶׁמֶשׁ וְיָרֵחַ;   הַלְלוּהוּ, כָּל-כּוֹכְבֵי אוֹר
ד.הַלְלוּהוּ, שְׁמֵי הַשָּׁמָיִם;   וְהַמַּיִם, אֲשֶׁר מֵעַל הַשָּׁמָיִם

Psalms 148:1-4 "Praise the Lord.[a]

*Praise the Lord from the heavens;
praise him in the heights above.
² Praise him, all his angels;
praise him, all his heavenly hosts.
³ Praise him, sun and moon;
praise him, all you shining stars.
⁴ Praise him, you highest heavens
and you waters above the skies".*

כט.מִבֶּטֶן מִי, יָצָא הַקָּרַח;   וּכְפֹר שָׁמַיִם, מִי יְלָדוֹ
ל.כָּאֶבֶן, מַיִם יִתְחַבָּאוּ;   וּפְנֵי תְהוֹם, יִתְלַכָּדוּ

> *Job 38:29 From whose womb comes the ice?*
> *Who gives birth to the frost from the heavens*
> *[30] when the waters become hard as stone,*
> *when the surface of the deep is frozen.*

Kent Hovind actually did a lecture which also gives support to the Canopy theory. He quoted a Newspaper article from 1993 entitled "New Theory is that a Lack of Oxygen Killed the Dinosaurs"- *International Falls, Minnesota News*

He goes on and shows an Apotosaurus.

This dinosaur is over 80 feet long, but has nostrils that are the same size as those found on a horse. In order for him to have survived, the oxygen content on earth had to have been much greater.

Do you remember this amber crystal from Jurassic Park? Well it is based off a real one. In the real crystal, there is a tiny air bubble which researchers tested. They discovered that it contained 31% oxygen, double the oxygen today. This is how the dinosaurs survived; today our air only contains 21%. Scientist say at 31% oxygen, humans could live over a 1000 years and run longer and faster than horses. I will prove, in a later scroll that dinosaurs and humans co-existed.

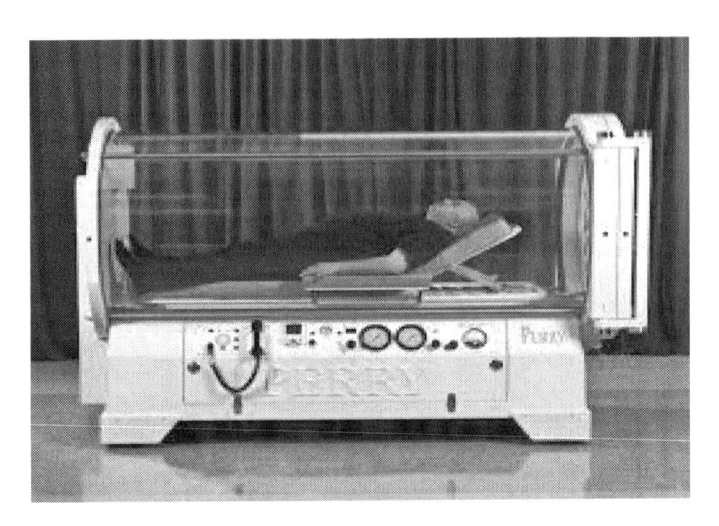

Ask your wealthy athletes about this. This is what you call a Hyperbaric Chamber. The large amount of oxygen in the tank allows the athlete to recover quickly and heal faster.

Now let us go back in the Torah and learn about NoakhHaTzaddik (the righteous).

אֵלֶּה, תּוֹלְדֹת נֹחַ--נֹחַ אִישׁ צַדִּיק תָּמִים הָיָה, בְּדֹרֹתָיו : אֶת-הָאֱלֹהִים, הִתְהַלֶּךְ-נֹחַ

Genesis 6:9 This is the account of Noah and his family. Noah was a righteous man, blameless among the people of his time, and he walked faithfully with God.

Noakh, who was taught by higher forces, understood what we now call Epigenetics. What is epigenetics? It is the study of what affects genes externally. Epigenetics has shown that environmental factors affect characteristics of organisms. These changes are sometimes passed on to the offspring. We must understand that the things we see or hear in our environment affect our subconscious. Our subconscious then records and plays back what it hears when we encounter a similar situation. The scriptures teach us to be aware of our surroundings if we want to connect to our Divine source.

אַשְׁרֵי הָאִישׁ-- אֲשֶׁר לֹא הָלַךְ, בַּעֲצַת רְשָׁעִים
וּבְדֶרֶךְ חַטָּאִים, לֹא עָמָד, וּבְמוֹשַׁב לֵצִים, לֹא יָשָׁב.

Psalms 1:1 "1 Blessed is the man that walketh not in the counsel of the ungodly, nor standeth in the way of sinners, nor sitteth in the seat of the scornful."

When dealing with epigenetics and the Tanakh, we must pull back the Peshat(simple) layer to get to the physiological meanings. I will show you how. Let us go to the Book of Numbers/B'midbar, 13th chapter, 4th verse. Here is where our Prophet Moses sent out spies to the Land, at the Lord's command, from the Desert of Paran. All of them were leaders of the Israelites. These are their names: לְמַטֵּה רְאוּבֵן, שַׁמּוּעַ בֶּן-זַכּוּר"*from the tribe of Reuben, Shammua son of Zakkur*". Keep in mind the twelve tribes represent a variation of things. They can represent the twelve zodiac signs, the twelve cranial nerves in the brain, or the twelve faculties of the human body. In this case let's focus on the latter. This Parashat deals with psychology, physiology and epigenetics. Verse four speaks of a man from the tribe of Rueben/Re'uven. Rueben represents the EYE because Rueben means 'to see a son'. Infact, if you add up the name it is 259, to bring it to single digits you add 2+5+9 and you will get 7. In iridology, there are 7 circles that are linked to different organs in the body.

Figure 6

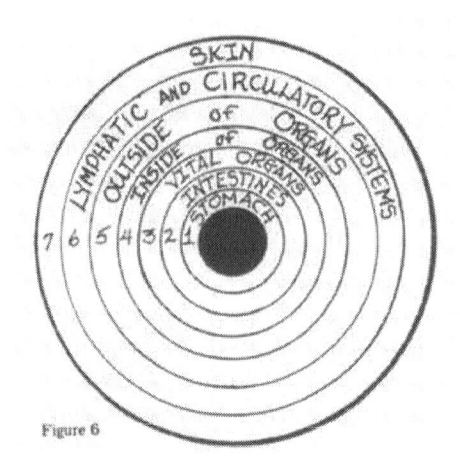

Seven principal colors also pass through the iris. All of this supports our understanding that Reuben symbolizes the Eye. Let us look at the spy that is representing, Reuben the Eye. His name is Shammua ben Zakkur. Shammua means to record and Zakkur means to reflect and playback. Isn't this what the eyes do? RECORD AND SEND A SIGNAL TO THE BRAIN TO PLAY BACK!

1. Light rays enter the eyes by passing through the cornea, the aqueous, the pupil, the lens, and vitreous, before striking the light sensitive nerve cells (rods and cones) in the retina.

2. Visual processing begins at the retina. Light energy produces chemical changes in the retina's light sensitive cells. These cells, in turn, produce electrical activity.

3. Nerve fibers from each cell join at the back of the eye to form the optic nerve.

4. The optic nerve of each eye meets the other at the optic chiasm. Medial nerves of each optic nerves cross, but lateral nerves stay on the same side. The overlap of nerve fibers allow for depth perception.

5. Electrical impulses are communicated to the visual cortex of the brain by way of the optic nerve.

6. The visual cortex makes sense of the electrical impulses, and either files the information for future reference or sends a message to a motor area for action. For a further break down, go to abiltypath.org

Now we will go to the next verse: לְמַטֵּה שִׁמְעוֹן, שָׁפָט בֶּן־חוֹרִי [5]"*from the tribe of Simeon, Shaphat son of Hori"*. Simeon/Shimone (שִׁמְעוֹן) is related to the the Hebrew word Shema (שְׁמַע) which means to hear or obey. Can you guess which faculty this represents? You guessed it, the EAR. Shaphat/שָׁפָט means governed, judged or discernment. What you hear develops your discernment. Hori/חוֹרִי is a cave. A cave symbolizes the subconscious of the mind but Hori also means to imprison. What you listen to develops your discernment by going into your subconscious. This will either incarcerate or liberate you.

    This portion of Noakh deals with spiritual liberation from this mental conditioning, liberation from those who have Cain like minds. Noakh/Noah(נֹחַ) means "at rest" and to get a more in depth meaning we are going to look at the meaning from the paleo-Hebrew. Noakh is spelled with a Nun and a Chet.

Name	Pictograph	Meaning	Name	Pictograph	Meaning
Aleph		Ox / strength / leader	Lamed		Staff / goad / control / "toward"
Bet		House / "In"	Mem		Water / chaos
Gimmel		Foot / camel / pride	Nun		Seed / fish / activity / life
Dalet		Tent door / pathway	Samekh		Hand on staff / support / prop
Hey		Lo! Behold! "The"	Ayin		Eye / to see / experience
Vav		Nail / peg / add / "And"	Pey		Mouth / word / speak
Zayin		Plow / weapon / cut off	Tsade		Man on side / desire / need
Chet		Tent wall / fence / separation	Qof		Sun on horizon / behind
Tet		Basket / snake / surround	Resh		Head / person / first
Yod		Arm and hand / work / deed	Shin		Eat / consume / destroy
Kaf		Palm of hand / to open	Tav		Mark / sign / covenant

The Nun is a seed representing growth and the Chet is a wall representing isolation. Combine the two and you have growth through isolation, which is meditation. What is meditation? Your mind "at rest"... Noakh! Noakh's numerical value is 58. In ancient Aztec's and Meso-American beliefs this number was seen as a sign that foreshadowed eminent destruction and judgment on mankind.

עֲשֵׂה לְךָ תֵּבַת עֲצֵי-גֹפֶר, קִנִּים תַּעֲשֶׂה אֶת-הַתֵּבָה; וְכָפַרְתָּ אֹתָהּ מִבַּיִת וּמִחוּץ, בַּכֹּפֶר

Make yourself an ark of gopher wood. Make rooms in the ark, and cover it inside and out with pitch Genesis 6:14

I will show you how this relates to meditation. Meditation sparks a certain Energy; in martial arts it's called Chi; in Hindu/India it's the Prana/Kundalii; in Hebrew its Chai/Aaron. Chi is emptiness and a readiness to receive all things. In the story of Noah (mind at rest) God tells him to make, for himself, an ark. The Hebrew word for ark is teibah /תֵּבָה (an empty vessel). See how the word teibah /תֵּבָה (an empty vessel) fits perfectly with Chi, meaning emptiness, or ready to receive? The ark was also made of gopher wood. In Hebrew, its etzey gopher/עֲצֵי־גֹפֶר. This is an unknown wood, but the words can also be

translated to mean divine counsel. It also related to the word גופרית, which means sulfur. Etzey or Etz, comes from the root word meaning tree or wood. Sulfur is a burning agent. This hints to the burning bush, which alludes to the seven chakras (see Exodus 25:31-40 & Exodus 3:1-5).

The parashah also says "pitch it... with pitch"/וְכָפַרְתָּ..בַּכֹּפֶר (Genesis 6:14). The Hebrew word for pitch (kofer/כֹּפֶר) is related to the word, Kippur/ רכפ (atonement). On Yom Kippur, we fast to repent. In Hebrew, repentance is T'shuva. Pitch (or in our intepretation of the tale, T'shuva, kippor/atonement) blocks out the Mabul/מַבּוּל (flood). Mabul derives from the Hebrew word balal/בָּלַל which means confusion. Meditation blocks out negative frequencies and or filters out subconscious thoughts. T'shuva, in the Hebraic spiritual system, is one of the most powerful tools that exist; to understand it, you must know the purpose of time.

In his book *Kabbalah on Sleep*, Yehuda Berg shows how time creates an illusion by putting a separation between cause and effect. The Tanakh speaks of this in Ecclesiastes 8:11: ‎אֲשֶׁר אֵין-נַעֲשָׂה פִתְגָם, מַעֲשֵׂה הָרָעָה מְהֵרָה; עַל-כֵּן מָלֵא לֵב בְּנֵי-הָאָדָם, בָּהֶם--לַעֲשׂוֹת רָע‎ "because sentence against an evil work is not executed speedily, therefore the heart of the sons of men is fully set in them to do evil." When we commit a sin, the effect doesn't usually smack us immediately. This is why you assume you are getting away clean, negating (in your mind at least) the fact that karma will come. The Hebrew word for it is Tiqqun. Our true power, however, lies in the fact that the same thing that creates this illusion is the same tool that can be used for mercy. When the sin (the cause) is committed, the time between cause and effect can be utilized for repentance. This can lighten the effect, or completely alleviate the repercussion.

Let us be honest, without us changing our lives and mastering self, then this whole spill about kundalini energy and pineal glands is reverted back into just fairytales. It's no more useful than the *Jack and the Bean Stalk story*.

Kundalini Energy

וְזֶה, אֲשֶׁר תַּעֲשֶׂה אֹתָהּ: שְׁלֹשׁ מֵאוֹת אַמָּה, אֹרֶךְ הַתֵּבָה, חֲמִשִּׁים אַמָּה רָחְבָּהּ, וּשְׁלֹשִׁים אַמָּה קוֹמָתָהּ

Genesis 6:15 "15 This is how you are to build it: The ark is to be three hundred cubits long, fifty cubits wide and thirty cubits high."

    Ok, let us break down these measurements. First we will start out with the word cubit, which is approximately 18 inches, 1+8=9. The number 9 resonates with consciousness and the role of being a light-bearer; one who found his spiritual path by being a humanitarian. Again self-mastery is the first step to finding your God consciousness. The number 300 correlates with the Hebrew letter Sheen, which denotes chewing, eating or destroying. In Kabbalistic wisdom, Sheen is seen as a Divine fire (in scriptures, when fire consumes the Hebrew word Akal/אָכַל is used, it means to eat). Fifty is represented by the Hebrew letter Nun and it is depicted as a seed sprouting upwards. Thirty is a shepherd's staff pointing upward to God who wields this staff. In ancient spiritual systems a staff represented the spine. Combine these and we have fire that sprouts up the spine, this is known as Kundalini or Aaron's rod. Your spine and brain is the staff of God. On the physical level the mystery reveals itself in the flow of cerebrospinal fluid (also known as liquid light or fire) that is in and around the brain and spine. In the cerebrospinal fluid (CSF) there is a highly concentrated amount of neuropeptides. Neuropeptides are "messenger molecules". We will get back to this in a second.

Let's focus on the CSF. CSF is clear and its chemical composition is similar to seawater (Noah's flood). This liquid supplies nutrients and eliminates waste. The spine is the central flow of energy and has highly conductive fluid.

    Neuropeptides, which are carried by the CSF, are the messenger molecules that send information and coordinate life in the cellular realm. This biochemical is highly concentrated in our limbic system and has dominion over our emotions. Neuropeptides are ligands, which are binders that bind to the receptor of a cell. A neuropeptide transmits a message to the cells and governs the functioning of the body organs, tissues etc. There are over a hundred of these neuropeptides that circulate in the body. The Tanakh alludes to this....

וַיְהִי בְּהַכְרִית אִיזֶבֶל, אֵת נְבִיאֵי יְהוָה; וַיִּקַּח עֹבַדְיָהוּ מֵאָה נְבִיאִים, וַיַּחְבִּיאֵם חֲמִשִּׁים אִישׁ בַּמְּעָרָה, וְכִלְכְּלָם, לֶחֶם וָמָיִם

1st Kings 18:4 " 4And when Jezebel cut off the prophets of the Yah, ObadiYah took a hundred prophets and hid them by fifties in a cave and fed them with bread and water."

What are prophets, aren't they messengers? Provided that ObadiYah means servant of Yah/God, they(prophets) were hidden from that which can be seen. All of our behavior and emotions are defined by microscopic physiological changes on a cellular level! Oh yeah and the two caves are your spine and limbic system where the prophet/neuropeptides are concentrated in.

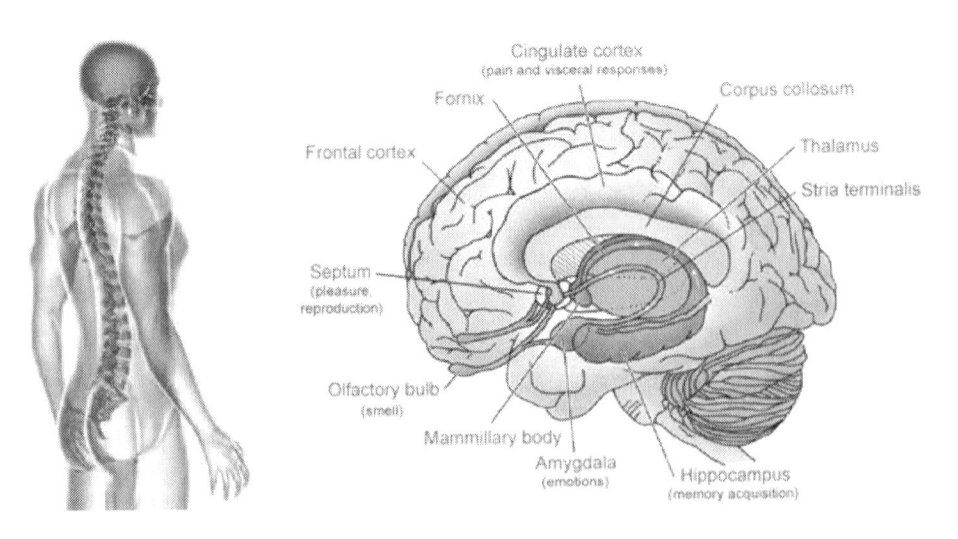

Breathing techniques and meditation are ways to increase the flow of cerebrospinal fluid. Neuropeptides in CSF are considered to be the 'keys', and the cell receptors are the 'locks'. These techniques create an increased flow of cerebrospinal fluid, allowing the neuropeptides to bind cells, and 'unlock' the dormant abilities and strengths inside you. This process enhances the cell life and even your life. When deep constant breathing patterns are performed, a life force is said to enter the body. How does the flow work? Well, from the brain to the base of the spine a pumping happens; from the top of the cranium to the sacrum, at the base of the spine. The pump at the base of the spine that distributes CSF sacral fluid is ignited by breathing from your diaphragm. Imagine your spine pumping fluid like a well pump, and the joints between the vertebrae of the spine act as pistons. Neuropeptides circulating in the brain and spine bring harmony between mind body and soul. It creates a magnetic field that's connected to everything. You see the Oneness of everything from the right side of the brain which is God consciousness.

שְׁמַע, יִשְׂרָאֵל: יְהוָה אֱלֹהֵינוּ, יְהוָה אֶחָד

Deuteronomy 6:4 "⁴Hear, O Israel: The Lord our God, the Lord is one!"

    The blissful feeling you get when your CSF is circulating strongly is from the serotonin that is secreted into the CSF. Serotonin itself is a neuropeptide that comes from the ependymal cell lining the ventricles of the brain where the cerebrospinal fluid is produced in large quantity.

    The pineal gland connects us to rhythms of life. Its main function is a circadian rhythm pacemaker. Circadian rhythm is any biological process that displays an endogenous, untrainable oscillation of about 24 hours. It regulates serotonin and melatonin secretions. When the CSF flow is increased, the pineal gland, which is bathed in cerebrospinal fluid, increases its production at night. This is important because the pineal gland produces melanin.

The Kundalini, which means "tangled", is the dormant energy at the base of the spine. Aaron(אַהֲרֹן) comes from the Hebrew word Ohair (אוהיר) also means tangled or interwoven. This energy is the electromagnetic field that surrounds the spine when the sodium, potassium, and other electrolytes in the CSF are being pumped upward and downward. It coils up the spine like a serpent. This is why you see "Aaron's rod" always turning into a serpent. Also in the Bible, we see different kinds of angels, like the Cherubim and Seraphim. In the Hebrew language, angels are called Mal'akhiym, which means messengers. Cherubim become cerebrum in Latin which is the brain. Seraphim means fiery serpent which is the energy from the spine traveling up to the cerebrum. Inside the spine, we have neuropeptides which are "messenger molecules". The Torah cannot be denied!

For more on CSF, look up an article called "The Soul Swims in the CSF" by Dr. Don Glassey.

Noah Was 600

ו וְנֹחַ, בֶּן-שֵׁשׁ מֵאוֹת שָׁנָה; וְהַמַּבּוּל הָיָה, מַיִם עַל-הָאָרֶץ. ז וַיָּבֹא נֹחַ, וּבָנָיו וְאִשְׁתּוֹ וּנְשֵׁי-בָנָיו אִתּוֹ--אֶל-הַתֵּבָה

    Genesis 7:6 "Noah was six hundred years old when the floodwaters came on the earth. And Noah and his sons and his wife and his sons' wives entered the ark to escape the waters of the flood"

Joanne , in Sacred Scribes, says the following about 600 :

    The number 600 is a compilation of the attributes and vibrations of the number G, and the energies and qualities of the powerful number 0 which appears twice, amplifying its influences. Number 6 offers the energies of love, home, family, empathy, sympathy, responsibility and reliability, care and nurturing, simplicity, and compromise. The number 6 also relates to provision and the material aspects of life, finding solutions and problem-solving. The number 0 resonates with the attributes of eternity and infinity, continuing cycles and flow, the beginning point. Number 0 stands for potential and/or choice, and represents the beginning of a spiritual journey and highlights the uncertainties that may entail. It encourages developing spirituality, and suggests that you listen to your intuition and higher-self as this is where you will find your answers.

Angel Number Joanne is a website that breakdown numerical numbers. It is shows that 600 is a positive message that deals with your home and family life, as well as the monetary and material world. It is a reminder that all supply comes from the Universe. Give any fears or concerns about your financial and material needs to the angels for healing and transmutation and allow a steady flow of abundance to enter your life. Accept the benevolence of the Universe's Energies and expect many blessings to enter your life. Know that you, your family and loved ones are well supported and protected, and all of your daily needs will be met in Divine order and in Divine time.

Ok, let's also keep in mind, the flood water is negative from the outside, representing confusion. On the inside, however, it represents the flow of CSF and the rise of kundalini, remember earlier the explanation that cerebrospinal fluid is like sea waters (hint, hint....).

In order for the spiritual transformation to work you have to become sympathetic, compassionate, and nurturing to those around you. Next, you must put your trust in the Infinite Power and remove all your fears. Let go! Concerns/fears are just false images placed into the mind by the subconscious.

ח מִן-הַבְּהֵמָה, הַטְּהוֹרָה, וּמִן-הַבְּהֵמָה, אֲשֶׁר אֵינֶנָּה טְהֹרָה; וּמִן-הָעוֹף--וְכֹל אֲשֶׁר-רֹמֵשׂ, עַל-הָאֲדָמָה. ט שְׁנַיִם שְׁנַיִם בָּאוּ אֶל-נֹחַ, אֶל-הַתֵּבָה--זָכָר וּנְקֵבָה: כַּאֲשֶׁר צִוָּה אֱלֹהִים, אֶת-נֹחַ. י וַיְהִי, לְשִׁבְעַת הַיָּמִים; וּמֵי הַמַּבּוּל, הָיוּ עַל-הָאָרֶץ. יא בִּשְׁנַת שֵׁשׁ-מֵאוֹת שָׁנָה, לְחַיֵּי-נֹחַ, בַּחֹדֶשׁ הַשֵּׁנִי, בְּשִׁבְעָה-עָשָׂר יוֹם לַחֹדֶשׁ--בַּיּוֹם הַזֶּה, נִבְקְעוּ כָּל-מַעְיְנוֹת תְּהוֹם רַבָּה, וַאֲרֻבֹּת הַשָּׁמַיִם, נִפְתָּחוּ. יב וַיְהִי הַגֶּשֶׁם, עַל-הָאָרֶץ, אַרְבָּעִים יוֹם, וְאַרְבָּעִים לָיְלָה. יג בְּעֶצֶם הַיּוֹם הַזֶּה בָּא נֹחַ, וְשֵׁם-וְחָם וָיֶפֶת בְּנֵי-נֹחַ; וְאֵשֶׁת נֹחַ, וּשְׁלֹשֶׁת נְשֵׁי-בָנָיו אִתָּם--אֶל-הַתֵּבָה. יד הֵמָּה וְכָל-הַחַיָּה לְמִינָהּ, וְכָל-הַבְּהֵמָה לְמִינָהּ, וְכָל-הָרֶמֶשׂ הָרֹמֵשׂ עַל-הָאָרֶץ, לְמִינֵהוּ; וְכָל-הָעוֹף לְמִינֵהוּ, כֹּל צִפּוֹר כָּל-כָּנָף. טו וַיָּבֹאוּ אֶל-נֹחַ, אֶל-הַתֵּבָה, שְׁנַיִם שְׁנַיִם מִכָּל-הַבָּשָׂר, אֲשֶׁר-בּוֹ רוּחַ חַיִּים. טז וְהַבָּאִים, זָכָר וּנְקֵבָה מִכָּל-בָּשָׂר בָּאוּ, כַּאֲשֶׁר צִוָּה אֹתוֹ, אֱלֹהִים; וַיִּסְגֹּר יְהוָה, בַּעֲדוֹ.

Genesis 7:8-16 "8 Pairs of clean and unclean animals, of birds and of all creatures that move along the ground, 9 male and female, came to Noah and entered the ark, as God had commanded Noah. 10 And after the seven days the floodwaters came on the earth. 11 In the six hundredth year of Noah's life, on the seventeenth day of the second month--on that day all the springs of the great deep burst forth, and the floodgates of the heavens were opened. 12 And rain fell on the earth forty days and forty nights. 13 On that very day Noah and his sons, Shem, Ham and Japheth, together with his wife and the wives of his three sons, entered the ark. 14 They had with them every wild animal according to its kind, all livestock according to their kinds, every creature that moves along the ground according to its kind and every bird according to its kind, everything with wings. 15 Pairs of all creatures that have the breath of life in them came to Noah and entered the ark. 16 The animals going in were male and female of every living thing, as God had commanded Noah. Then the LORD shut him in."

The 2 of each kind, male and female represents positive and negative energy which, as we explained earlier, creates a magnetic field. Also in the ark, there are 3 classes of creatures, which correspond to the 3 different parts of our brain: cattle (mammalian), creeping things (reptilian), and fowl (cortex). The reptilian part of the brain is the oldest. It is compulsive, impulsive, and involuntary. It's about self and doesn't learn from its mistakes and repeats them.

The mammalian part of the brain is connected to emotion and feelings. It establishes values according to an emotional standpoint. These 2 parts make up what we call the subconscious.

Now the cortex is the conscious mind, gathering its discernment by the use of rational interpretations of experience. The human brain is far more creative than any computer.

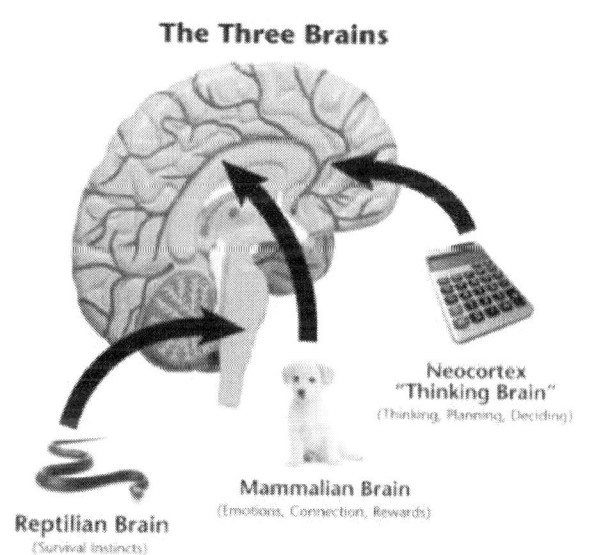

The Three Brains

Neocortex
"Thinking Brain"
(Thinking, Planning, Deciding)

Mammalian Brain
(Emotions, Connection, Rewards)

Reptilian Brain
(Survival Instincts)

The conscious mind deals with sight. The subconscious is blind and deals with sensory input. This is why the subconscious mind deals with imaginary and reality in the same way. Have you ever watched a movie and someone is killed and you cry, even though consciously you know they are actors and they are really alive? This is because our subconscious doesn't know the difference between what's real and what's fake.

Most conscious thoughts come from an inner voice which is connected to vocabulary. A large vocabulary is good at exercising your cortex. The reptilian and mammalian portions of your brain are limited when dealing with vocabulary. This is why cursing is dangerous. It exercises the impulsive part of the brain, slowing down and at times causing a regression of, cognitive development.

Sirach 23:12 There is one way of speaking that is like death itself-may no Israelite ever be guilty of it! Devout people do not wallow in such sin, and they will keep away from such behavior.

Sirach 23:13 Don't fall into the habit of course, profane talk; it is sinful.

Sirach 23:14 You might forget yourself while in the company of important people and make a fool of yourself with some foul word that comes to you naturally. Think how your parents would feel! You would curse the day you were born and wish you were dead!

Sirach 23:15 If you fall into the habit of using offensive language, you will never break yourself of it as long as you live

Everything gets into your subconscious, but your conscious acts as a filter. The conscious mind starts to develop in a child at age 3, and is fully developed at 20, but that does not mean we utilize it the way we are supposed to. In the Hebrew language, the number 20 is represented by a Kaf which is a palm denoting submission. It also denotes grasping the force. In the Mayan tradition, the number 20 represents the god Solar, the energy from the sun. Samson, in the Bible, (whose name actually means Solar) reigned for how long? You guessed it 20 years! This sends us to the solar plexus chakra which is located at the navel. This chakra deals with power, self-esteem, self-image, energy, will and responsibility.

The Chakras

Numbers in the Torah are the beginning of decoding the words of the ancients. Numbers are a universal code and breaks all language barriers. The Most High told Noah to take seven clean animals. He also spoke to Noah 7 days before the flood.

ב מִכֹּל הַבְּהֵמָה הַטְּהוֹרָה, תִּקַּח-לְךָ שִׁבְעָה שִׁבְעָה--אִישׁ וְאִשְׁתּוֹ; וּמִן-הַבְּהֵמָה אֲשֶׁר לֹא טְהֹרָה הִוא, שְׁנַיִם--אִישׁ וְאִשְׁתּוֹ. ג גַּם מֵעוֹף הַשָּׁמַיִם שִׁבְעָה שִׁבְעָה, זָכָר וּנְקֵבָה, לְחַיּוֹת זֶרַע, עַל-פְּנֵי כָל-הָאָרֶץ. ד כִּי לְיָמִים עוֹד שִׁבְעָה, אָנֹכִי מַמְטִיר עַל-הָאָרֶץ, אַרְבָּעִים יוֹם, וְאַרְבָּעִים לָיְלָה; וּמָחִיתִי, אֶת-כָּל-הַיְקוּם אֲשֶׁר עָשִׂיתִי, מֵעַל, פְּנֵי הָאֲדָמָה

Genesis 7:2-4 "2 Of every clean beast thou shalt take to thee by sevens, the male and his female: and of beasts that are not clean by two, the male and his female. 3 Of fowls also of the air by sevens, the male and the female; to keep seed alive upon the face of all the earth. 4 For yet seven days, and I will cause it to rain upon the earth forty days and forty nights; and every living substance that I have made will I destroy from off the face of the earth."

The funny thing about these 7's and the correlation with chakras is that it is in chapter 7. The 7 chakras are energy centers up the spine that are near the endocrine glands in the human body. These energy centers create your aura.

The number 7 is powerful in the Scriptures; most people will chalk it up to coincidence. I don't believe in coincidence.

1. The **Root chakra** is at the base of the spine where the kundalini is said to be dormant. It is wrapped around the spine 3 and a half times. Its color is red which deals with desire, lust and sex. When one has

unbalance in that area, they have trust issues from an early age. Hint: the root chakra is the root of all problems….

2. The **Sacral chakra** is placed between the navel and the genitals. It deals with expression, creativity, masculine/feminine energy and emotions. The color is orange and its element is water which denotes semen; the water of life.

3. The **Solar Plexus Chakra** deals with power, self-esteem, self-image, energy will and responsibility. Now remember; Samson represents solar energy. When the Philistines guess Samson's riddle, he became angry and tied together 300 foxes and strapped torches on them to burn down the village. Again, 300 is the sheen that correlates with fire, 3+0+0= 3 representing the third chakra. The number 3, appears even at the end of Samson's life. When Samson killed himself and the people in the arena, there were 3000 on the roof.

4. The **Heart chakra** is the medium chakra. If it's mastered, it brings balance to your other chakras. This chakra vibrates to the color emerald, and is strengthened through love. Its shape is like the Shield of David. This chakra is called "Anahata" but sometimes, it is called Dvadashadala. Do you see David in that name? This chakra is the Merkaba which is the chariot, or throne of God.

5. The **Throat Chakra** deals with communication, manifestation and carries the frequency of blue.

…וְרוּחַ אֱלֹהִים, מְרַחֶפֶת עַל-פְּנֵי הַמָּיִם. ג וַיֹּאמֶר אֱלֹהִים, יְהִי אוֹר; וַיְהִי-אוֹר

Genesis 1:2-3 "…..And the spirit of God hovered above the waters 3 God said "let there be light" and there was light"

Water is represented by the color blue. This is where you get the names Bluetooth, which you communicate with, and Blue ray DVD.

6. The **Third eye chakra** is also known as Ajna chakra or the pineal gland. It is seen as a double lotus.

וּשְׁתַּיִם דְּלָתוֹת, לַדְּלָתוֹת: שְׁתַּיִם, מוּסַבּוֹת דְּלָתוֹת--שְׁתַּיִם לְדֶלֶת אֶחָת, וּשְׁתֵּי דְלָתוֹת לָאַחֶרֶת

Ezekiel 41:24 "a double door, and each door had two swinging leaves: two for the one door and two such leaves for the other"

The pineal gland is located in the hypothalamus and has a pine shape. This gland regulates the melatonin which makes us sleepy. Your third eye actually has a retina and lens. Once the kundalini hits this chakra, it vibrates at a higher frequency, allowing you to see deeper in yourself and tap into the universal rhythms of the world. This heightens your intuition and also allows your body to heal itself. Its color frequency is indigo.

7. The **Crown chakra** is the highest level where you are in the astral plane and in a state of bliss. It is said to be your own place of connection to God, the Chakra of Divine purpose and personal destiny. Blockage can manifest as psychological problems. It's also known as the thousand petal lotus. In the Hebrew language, it is the Keter, the highest of the sephirot of the Tree of Life in Kabbalah. It is said to be incomprehensible to man.

Noachian 40 Day Meditation

....נִבְקְעוּ כָּל-מַעְיְנֹת תְּהוֹם רַבָּה, וַאֲרֻבֹּת הַשָּׁמַיִם, נִפְתָּחוּ. יב וַיְהִי הַגֶּשֶׁם, עַל-הָאָרֶץ, אַרְבָּעִים יוֹם, וְאַרְבָּעִים לָיְלָה

Genesis 7:11-12 "All the fountains of the great deep burst apart, And the flood gates of the sky broke open. 12 the rain fell upon the earth forty days and forty nights."

Although factual, this also alludes to the pumping of liquid from the sacral and the cranium. 40 is as powerful number In ancient times, it deals with the four levels of consciousness: Reason, Order, Measurement and Judgment. Judgment can also be understood as Mental, Emotional, Physical and Spiritual law. In ancient spiritual systems, a 40 day meditation was known to break bad habits. The number of days was a sacred time period in the Bible for enacting change. If you are consistent, it will clear your subconscious and set up new positive patterns.

The benefits of meditation were discussed in an article by Jon Lieff, M.D. Entitled*Meditation and Brain Changes: Recent Research and Applications*. This article additionally describes the severe stress caused by the increase in some regions of the amygdala, (emotional center, related to fear) and decrease in regions of the hippocampus (memory and learning), and prefrontal cortex (decision making). It notes that meditation counteracts these stress related brain changes. Meditation decreases anxiety and fear, and increases memory and cognitive abilities.

The neuroscience review also reported that compassion meditation (summarized in the previous post and below) increases gamma oscillations and synchronythese are rhythms that are commonly observed in many brain regions during both waking and sleep states, as well as increased activity in brain regions dealing with empathy. It also emphasized that changes in the brain from meditation can occur in just eight weeks.

The number 40 correlates with Mem. In the ancient Hebrew pictograph, it is a logogram of water. Water is a powerful element in prayer.

Here is a quote for HaShar of A.O.C., "Water is indeed an absolute phenomenal gift and sign of the Creator's mere existence. A single fertilized egg is 96% water, at birth 80% then through childhood on, the percentage drops and stabilizes at 70%, depending on one's health…." It's fascinating how we are surrounded by water in the womb and even when we leave the womb, we are still surrounded. Water comes in three forms: solid, liquid and gas. The very air we breathe is the gaseous form of water, proving we are still surrounded by water. This also proves that it's the most essential element to all kingdoms, plant, mineral, animal and man. Thought, memory, and words--whether good or bad--have a profound effect on us at a cellular level. This is simply because water is a transmitter and transporter within the cells of bodies. This is how we know prayer (which is our thoughts) and words are heard and answered. As they travel from the cellular level within, they become transmitted by water as it permeates without, eventually reaching the air as a gaseous form of water. They are then transported to the recipient who is prayed for. The process also works in reverse, from the air etcetera. So there is a scientific basis and methodology in which prayer works by way of water. It's no wonder why the Creator made it the most abundant and necessary element. In every important biblical narrative, water is the key player. From Noah and the flood, Moses parting the sea, and Yehoshua turning water to wine.

Noakh, Nephilim and the school of Shem

A question I always had was 'Who taught Noah?' Well hints are within the scriptures. Noah had three sons Shem, Ham and Japheth. When we look into their names we see that this is not the first time Shem is being used to name someone or something.

הַנְּפִלִים הָיוּ בָאָרֶץ, בַּיָּמִים הָהֵם, וְגַם אַחֲרֵי-כֵן אֲשֶׁר יָבֹאוּ בְּנֵי הָאֱלֹהִיּח אֶל-בְּנוֹת הָאָדָם, וְיָלְדוּ לָהֶם : הֵמָּה הַגִּבֹּרִים אֲשֶׁר מֵעוֹלָם, אַנְשֵׁי הַשֵּׁם

Genesis 6:4 "It was then, and later too, that the Nephilim (the fallen ones) appeared on earth, when the sons of Elohiym slept with the daughters of Adam, who bore them offspring. They were mighty ones from the universe (or eternity), men of the "Shem."
Let's see who are these men that came from the universe.

Book of Enoch 64:2 "These are the Angels who descended upon the earth and revealed what was hidden to the children of the people". Usually people out of gratitude or appreciation name their children after teachers, heroes or people who influenced their lives. Could it be that "the fallen ones"(הַנְּפִלִים) the men of the "Shem" taught the secrets of the "Shem"? Most translations for Shem are 'name' or 'reknown', but that is actually inaccurate. Let us add the definition 'epithet' (an adjective or descriptive phrase expressing a quality characteristic of the person or thing mention). Inside the *Ancient Hebrew Lexicon* by Jeff A. Benner, a more in-depth definition is given-- breath, wind or character. The root shem also appears in the word Shamayim/שָׁמַיִם, the Hebrew word for heaven. When we look into neighboring languages, such Akkadian, we see a similar word Shamu which means sky. We can take that and now look at "the men of the Shem", which takes on a new meaning such as the men of the breath/heavens who were from the universe and eternity. Could it be that these men, or angels, came down and taught man breathing techniques that connected them with the stars, and allowed them to bring heaven to earth? How else could the ancients understand the universe?

"For the purpose of being in a human body is to bring what you call heaven on to earth" -The Emerald Cathedral by Charlene Van Crump

During meditation you are taught to focus on the breath. When you focus on the breath, you connect to the inner soul. Deep down inside, you connect with the infinite or eternal YHWH. Our breath is connected to the physical and spiritual world; it's a link between the two. The Hebrew word for spirit and wind is Ruach. The breath is Neshama which is the essence of Elohiym connected to our soul, the nefesh.

וַיִּיצֶר יְהוָה אֱלֹהִים אֶת-הָאָדָם, עָפָר מִן-הָאֲדָמָה, וַיִּפַּח בְּאַפָּיו, נִשְׁמַת חַיִּים ; וַיְהִי הָאָדָם, לְנֶפֶשׁ חַיָּה

Genesis 2:7 "And YHWH, Elohiym, created man out of the dust of the earth, and blew into his nostrils the breath of life (nishmatchayiym) and man became a living soul (l'nefeshchayah)"

There is an article entitled The Soul, The Breath, and the Name of Yehowah by Melech ben Ya'aqov. In this article, he stumbles across a divine revelation "every breath we take is the word 'Yehowah'. If you open your lips slightly, sit up straight and breathe in and out deeply through our mouth, you will notice with each full cycle of breath, the word you are saying 'Yehowah'."

Our breath consists of three parts. The first part is when air is drawn through the mouth. The lips are slightly puckered, and the air flow is slightly constricted. This sound that is naturally created by this stage of breath is "Ye"(Try it you will see). After the initial flow of air is drawn in through the mouth, the second stage of the breath is characterized by the lowering of the diaphragm and an expansion of the lungs. The sound naturally created by this stage is "Ho". Finally once the lungs reach maximum expansion, exhalation commences. The sound naturally created by this stage is "Wa".

.... שְׁנַיִם שְׁנַיִם מִכָּל-הַבָּשָׂר, אֲשֶׁר-בּוֹ רוּחַ חַיִּים

Genesis 7:15 "Pairs of all creatures that have the breath of life in them came to Noah and entered the ark."

    Okay it is understood that the animals are breathing. Why didn't it just say all animals? Because the breath of life is breathing that adds life, it's specifically talking about breathing and meditation.

וַיָּשֻׁבוּ הַמַּיִם מֵעַל הָאָרֶץ, הָלוֹךְ וָשׁוֹב; וַיַּחְסְרוּ הַמַּיִם--מִקְצֵה, חֲמִשִּׁים וּמְאַת יוֹם

The water receded steadily from the earth. At the end of the hundred and fifty days the water had gone down. Genesis 8: 3

Let's dive into the significance of 150. One hundred fifty is what happens when you do 40 days of meditation, and the flooding of the cerebral spinal fluid. 1 represents new beginning and personal fulfillment. 5 represents life decisions, motivation, and resourcefulness.. 0 behind a number magnifies energies. After 40 days of meditation, it should influence your life and promote the consistent flow CSF/ (flood waters of the Noah story), giving you a new beginning to seek personal goals. This motivation is inspired by your new ability to perceive life from a positive perspective. You developed the ability to utilize things that destroyed you and create a foundation based on the inspiration and lessons enshrouded in what appeared to be a distraction.

Break down the number 150 a bit more in detail. Qoof is 100 which is the sun on the horizon. Noon is 50, which is the seed on sperm that represents growth.

I want to revisit the pineal gland and pituitary gland to give more meaning to the number 150. To perceive higher consciousness, the two glands must vibrate in unison. This happens during our meditation and sun gazing. Both bring us in tune with earth's magnetic field. In his article, *Endocrine Secretions during Sun Bathing* by Wayne Purdin states "the solar wind at dawn, charging the earth's magnetic field, stimulates the pineal gland. This is why the period between 4-6am is the best time to meditate and why sun rise is the best time to sun gaze. At this time, the pineal gland stimulates the pituitary gland to secrete human growth hormones." Wow. Now do you see all of the hidden messages in the number 150 (which is a quoof and nun) that symbolizes the sun on the horizon (dawn).

The Raven and the Dove

וַיְשַׁלַּח, אֶת-הָעֹרֵב; וַיֵּצֵא יָצוֹא וָשׁוֹב, עַד-יְבֹשֶׁת הַמַּיִם מֵעַל הָאָרֶץ

Genesis 8:7 " 7 And he sent forth a raven, which went forth to and fro, until the waters were dried up from off the earth."

The raven is the bird that feeds off the dead. In ancient times, ravens were messengers of God that symbolized death or deceit. In the Torah, this bird alludes to our negative past, which we trust in to give us messages which are actually deceitful. These messages also obscure our visions. Our negative thoughts feed off of negative energy and the magnetite in the brain attracts more negativity. Notice that the raven was the first to be trusted in our earlier years. We were-- and in many cases we still are--extremely vulnerable and our brains are very impressionable to traumatic events. We live our lives as a product of early childhood hurts, which leads us to believe that emotions are our intuition, protecting us from the evil in this world. But in truth, the raven in our ark (mind) is in fact the evil we should be fighting. In the Torah the raven never returned. This is because you do not own your negative energy, or thoughts. Negative behavior is of this world.

The dove is a symbol of peace, innocence, purity and faith. When you begin meditation, negative thoughts will emerge (Raven). With more practice you begin to feel pure bliss and innocence. In ParashatNoakh, the dove was sent out three times. During the last two times, Noah waits seven days in between. Let us stop right here. What is the portion hinting towards? Keep in mind that it says the dove returned. This leads me to understand that it's speaking of an internal circuit. To me the Torah is breaking down the microcosmic orbit meditation. "The microcosmic orbit is a meditation practice in which you focus on circulating your life force through 2 of the most important energy channels. The Functional Channel (Ren Mal), and the Governor Channel (Du Mal) connect in a flowing circle going up the spine, over the head and down the front center of the body. The front and back channel are joined to form a circuit of continuous energy flow. This circuit is called microcosmic orbiting."- The Flowingwheel!

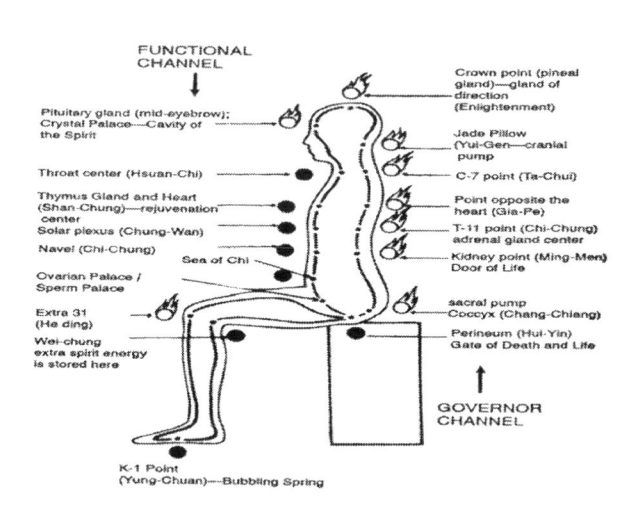

This is healing energy in us that also gives us strength and clarity. This Parashat (portion) is one of the most powerful in the Torah because it teaches us how to heal and protect ourselves from worldly influences. In meditation our mind finds a Holy Place.

תָּנַח הַתֵּבָה בַּחֹדֶשׁ הַשְּׁבִיעִי, בְּשִׁבְעָה-עָשָׂר יוֹם לַחֹדֶשׁ, עַל, הָרֵי אֲרָרָט

Genesis 8:4 "And the ark (mind) rested in the 7th month, on the 7th day of the month, upon the mountains of Ararat (holy place).

After your 40 day meditation there is a new beginning. Thus, Noakh, being 601, represents after the flood. The number 601 is divine assistance coming along in your life and the ability to create your own reality.Noakh building an altar represents the heart and love, slaughtering animalistic impulses.

אֶת-קַשְׁתִּי, נָתַתִּי בֶּעָנָן; וְהָיְתָה לְאוֹת בְּרִית, בֵּינִי וּבֵין הָאָרֶץ

Genesis 9:13 "I do set my bow in the cloud and it shall be a token of a covenant between me and the earth."

The Rainbow

The rainbow, according to the ancients, is a bridge to heaven. This multicolored stairway symbolizes the reunion between God and man. The rainbow corresponds to the color of our chakras: red, orange, yellow, green, blue, indigo, and violet. The familiar acronym is Roy G. Biv. Colors vibrate at different frequencies.

Color	Frequency
Red	400-484
Orange	484-508
Yellow	508-526
Green	526-606
Blue	606-670
Indigo	670-700
Violet	700-789

Our chakras vibrate to certain frequencies and respond to certain outside frequencies. The rainbow is said to be the bridge to heaven. So if, biblically, the rainbow means reunion between God and man, wouldn't the rainbow/ chakra be the covenant of salvation?

ח וַיִּהְיוּ בְנֵי-נֹחַ, הַיֹּצְאִים מִן-הַתֵּבָה--שֵׁם, וְחָם וָיָפֶת; וְחָם, הוּא אֲבִי כְנָעַן. יט שְׁלֹשָׁה אֵלֶּה, בְּנֵי-נֹחַ; וּמֵאֵלֶּה, נָפְצָה כָל-הָאָרֶץ. כ וַיָּחֶל נֹחַ, אִישׁ הָאֲדָמָה; וַיִּטַּע, כָּרֶם. כא וַיֵּשְׁתְּ מִן-הַיַּיִן, וַיִּשְׁכָּר; וַיִּתְגַּל, בְּתוֹךְ אָהֳלֹה. כב וַיַּרְא, חָם אֲבִי כְנַעַן, אֵת, עֶרְוַת אָבִיו; וַיַּגֵּד לִשְׁנֵי-אֶחָיו, בַּחוּץ. כג וַיִּקַּח שֵׁם וָיֶפֶת אֶת-הַשִּׂמְלָה, וַיָּשִׂימוּ עַל-שְׁכֶם שְׁנֵיהֶם, וַיֵּלְכוּ אֲחֹרַנִּית, וַיְכַסּוּ אֵת עֶרְוַת אֲבִיהֶם; וּפְנֵיהֶם, אֲחֹרַנִּית, וְעֶרְוַת אֲבִיהֶם, לֹא רָאוּ

Genesis 9:18-23

"¹⁸And the sons of Noah, that went forth of the ark, were Shem, and Ham, and Japheth: and Ham is the father of Canaan.
¹⁹These are the three sons of Noah: and of them was the whole earth overspread. ²⁰And Noah began to be an husbandman, and he planted a vineyard:²¹And he drank of the wine, and was drunken; and he was uncovered within his tent.²²And Ham, the father of Canaan, saw the nakedness of his father, and told his two brethren without.²³And Shem and Japheth took a garment, and laid it upon both their shoulders, and went backward, and covered the nakedness of their father; and their faces were backward, and they saw not their father's nakedness."

We will now look at the verses in Sanskrit from the Bhagavad Gita , which has some surprising similarities to with the Hebrew Tanakh.

In the portion of the Bhagavad Gita which parallels with the tale of the deluge in our parsha, Noah is Novak, which means 'navigator'; Shem is pronounced Soma, which is interpreted as 'secret liquor'; and Japheth is Japti, meaning procreation. Canaan, is pronounced Kamama which means 'lustfulness', or 'the eternal slave of drunkenness'. There are a few things we can extract from here. In the first 10 seconds of meditation, neurons go off like rockets, similar to the brain's reaction when sleep is occurring. These stimuli assist in reconstructing the mind. So if the ark is the mind at rest, what role does Novak play in the mind according to the Sanskrit words? The answer was revealed to me when I started studying neurons.

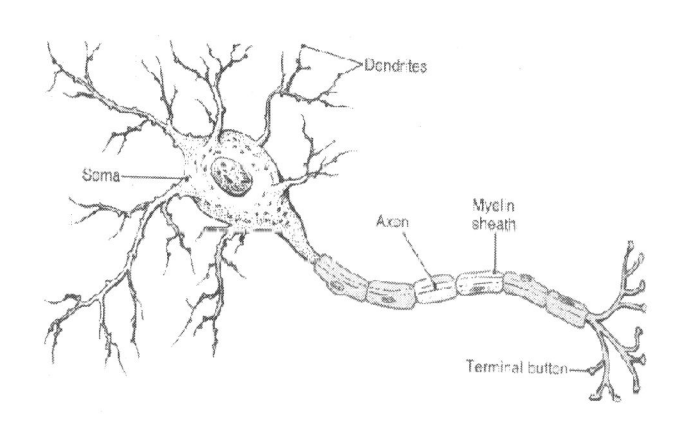

The cells of neurons have a nucleus which acts as a navigator (Novak) but what is mind blowing is the cell body that covers the nucleus/ Novak/Noah is called the "SOMA". Obviously, this is spelled just like 'Soma' in the Bhagavad Gita, corresponding to the Hebrew figure Shem. In simpler terms, Shem and Japheth covered noah, the novak/navigator or nucleus, the soma/shem (covering of the nucleus) and japta/japeth/procreation (are vital elements in what sustains (procreation) andprotects (cell covering) among the the nuclei of cells within neurons.

Uncovering God's Nakedness

There are many messages that can be taken from Noah. The final and the most powerful to me was something that was revealed to me while preparing my lesson for ParashatNoakh. I've seen many parallels between this parasha and the creation story. God hovered over the water, just as the ark hovered over the water before dry land appeared. The earth was then repopulated, which parallels with the culminating act of creation in which Adam was created. All of this leads me to believe that there is something about Noah that is explaining, or expounding upon the Divine King, the Holy one of Israel, blessed is He. It can be found in the place you would least expect it. In ParashatNoakh, let's say that Noah symbolizes the incorporeal King, YHWH ElohiymMelekhHaOlam. Melekh means 'King', Ha is 'the', and Olam means 'Eternity/ Universe'. Olam, the universe, comes from the Hebrew word Alam. Alam is translated as "hidden." So he is the infinite energy and the Ruler that is hidden in the universe. In The Book of Enoch, the angels taught the secret thing of the Lord. If Noah parallels to God in this story, wouldn't it be that Canaan uncovered the nakedness of God by teaching God's mysteries to those who are not worthy. Gabriel haTalmid Comments:

> " It is necessary to explain what is spoken of when the phrase 'nakedness of God' is mentioned. Heaven forbid that this is misunderstood to mean that God has nakedness such as that of man. God, unlike man, has no form, nor any body. In fact, if he did, this would violate his oneness, which is the central idea of our recital of the Shema. Rambam explains this very important concept perfectly in HilkhothYesodheiHattorah 1:5-7:

אלוה זה אחד הוא--אינו לא שניים ולא יתר על שניים, אלא אחד, שאין כייחודו אחד מן האחדים הנמצאים בעולם: לא אחד כמין שהוא כולל אחדים הרבה, ולא אחד כגוף שהוא נחלק למחלקות ולקצוות; אלא ייחוד שאין ייחוד אחר כמותו בעולם.

> This God is one--he is not two or more than two entities, but one, and there is nothing like his oneness found among [the various] unities in the universe. Not one according to a type/species of which there are many collective individuals, and not one like a body of which can be divided into divisions and pieces; rather a oneness such as His, is unlike any other oneness in the universe.

ואילו היו האלוהות הרבה--היו גופין וגוויות, מפני שאין הנמנין השווין במציאתן נפרדין זה מזה אלא במאורעין שיארעו הגופות והגוויות. ואילו היה היוצר גוף וגווייה--היה לו קץ ותכלית, שאי אפשר להיות גוף שאין לו קץ. וכל שיש לו קץ ותכלית, יש לכוחו קץ וסוף.

> Had there been many gods--they would have bodies and corporeality, for entities considered equal cannot be distinguished from one another except in bodily properties and corporeality. Thus it follows that what is of bodily and corporeal form---has an end and can be destroyed, for it is impossible for there to be a body that has no end. For everything that has an end and is capable of being destroyed, also has an end and limit regarding its power.

וא‑לוהינו ברוך שמו, הואיל וכוחו אין לו קץ ואינו פוסק, שהרי הגלגל סובב ונמשך, אין כוחו כוח גוף. והואיל ואינו גוף, לא יארעו מאורעות הגופות כדי שיהא נחלק ונפרד מאחר; לפיכך אי אפשר שיהיה אלא אחד. וידיעת דבר זה--מצוות עשה, שנאמר "ה' אלוהינו, ה' אחד" <u>דברים ד,</u>

> Since Our God blessed be his name, has strength without end or pause, of which perpetually guides the sphere, his strength is not bodily. Since he has no body, he has no bodily properties, which can be divided and separated from one another; therefore it is impossible for him to be anything but one. [To] know this

matter--[is] a positive commandment, as it is written "Hashem our God, Hashem is one" <u>Debharim/Dueteronomy 6:4</u>

Anthropomorphisms concerning God are used in hebraic thought to communicate symbolic and metaphorical truths. The Tanakh even uses anthropomorphisms when referring to things other than God. For example, verses such as Shemot/Exodus 10:5 (וְכִסָּה אֶת-עֵין הָאָרֶץ/and cover the eye of the land) and Tehillim/Psalms 98:8 (נְהָרוֹת יִמְחֲאוּ-כָף/the rivers clap their hands) are meant to be taken figuratively. They do not mean that rivers or land actually have feet or eyes. When the phrase 'nakedness of God' is used, it is also to be taken figuratively."

To give us further insight into what I mean when I use the phrase 'the nakedness of God', let's briefly look at the figurative use of nakedness in the Tanakh.

וַיִּזְכֹּר יוֹסֵף--אֵת הַחֲלֹמוֹת, אֲשֶׁר חָלַם לָהֶם; וַיֹּאמֶר אֲלֵהֶם מְרַגְּלִים אַתֶּם, לִרְאוֹת אֶת-עֶרְוַת הָאָרֶץ בָּאתֶם.

Genesis 42:9 Then he remembered his dreams about them and said to them, "You are spies! You have come to see where our land is unprotected.

כְּעַן, כָּל-קֳבֵל דִּי-מְלַח הֵיכְלָא מְלַחְנָא, וְעַרְוַת מַלְכָּא, לָא אֲרִיךְ-לַנָא לְמֶחֱזֵא; עַל-דְּנָה--שְׁלַחְנָא, וְהוֹדַעְנָא לְמַלְכָּא.

Ezra 4:14 Now since we are under obligation to the palace and it is not proper for us to see the king dishonored, we are sending this message to inform the king,

Both of the above verses have something in common in that both verses speak about nakedness. In Genesis, the phrase which is translated as 'where our land is unprotected' comes from the Hebrew which literally says עֶרְוַת הָאָרֶץ/the nakedness of the land. In Ezra, the verse which is translated as 'the king dishonored', comes from the Aramaic, which literally says עֲרְוַת מַלְכָּא / the nakedness of the king.

In both verses, the context shows that the concept of nakedness is not to be taken literally, but figuratively. Both come from the Semitic understanding of nakedness as a concept, signifying that which should not be seen. In Genesis, the accusation was that Joseph's brothers were attempting to ascertain the political weaknesses of the land which could be exploited. This was referred to as an attempt by Joseph's brothers to see the land's nakedness. In Ezra, it is dishonorable for the harm to come to king and his reputation, and this is referred to nakedness.

This prohibition against uncovering the Nakedness of God is even alluded to in *Psalm 25:14*

סוֹד יְהוָה, לִירֵאָיו; וּבְרִיתוֹ, לְהוֹדִיעָם

" The secret of the LORD is with them that fear him; and he will shew them his covenant."

Did we not see that one of his covenants was the rainbow/chakras? So what was Shem's role? Well... Shem covered up that which is reserved only for those initiated into the deeper aspects of the Torah. The Torah teaches the reverence of the eternal, moral and ethical laws which are the foundation of spirituality. On the surface the Torah is just historical stories and laws, but in truth, it is encoded with messages that will guide you and give you the ability to unlock the powers of the universe. If these secrets are in the hands of the unjust they will corruptly manipulate the masses by muses, genetic modification and altering frequencies. Without a foundation such as the Torah, he who journeys into the metaphysical realm without being upright creates a gateway to the flood waters of darkness. To extract the "Holy Technology" without being bound to the law will results in spiritual and mental desolation. The Divine spark deep in your soul fades. As your ego grows, it thrives off of the acquisition of

knowledge for personal gain. The reptilian and mammalian parts of the brain become stronger, causing a person to begin acting in more emotional and impulsive ways. You eventually become your own god and your views eventually become the only truth. Eventually those who surround you are only those who feed your ego. These people will be your cheerleaders down your path of darkness. As students, they will mimic your arrogance and perfect your corrupted craft. Eventually, what appears is cooperation that turns into an envious competition, destroying the very source that leads its disciples down the path of darkness.

    For this reason, the Mishna (Hagiga 2:1) warns those who study Torah. Ironically, matters of nakedness--in this case the laws of incest--, are juxtaposition to esoteric aspects of the Torah. The Mishna prohibits the teaching of these matters in public. Even when they were expounded in private, it was only to the wise. This is the case because the laws of incest, just as the maaseib'reshith(the mysteries of Creation), and the maaseimerkabha (the mysterries of the chariot), could all lead the unwise to have inappropriate, or even idolotrous thoughts. This is why the Mishna ends this particular section with the warning: וכל שלא חס על כבוד קונו, רתוי לו כאילו לא בא לעולם /"And all who have no honor for their Creator(owner) it would have mercy upon him to not have come into existence".

Astronomical Breakdown of Noah

The legend of Noah's Flood begins in Aquarius during the astrological age of Taurus. It follows the sun's ecliptic path from Aquarius, to Pisces, to Aries, to Taurus, and to Gemini. For further reference, see Eden to Babel *and a* Map of the Zodiac.

Noah personifies Aquarius, the Waterman.

ט אֵלֶּה, תּוֹלְדֹת נֹחַ--נֹחַ אִישׁ צַדִּיק תָּמִים הָיָה, בְּדֹרֹתָיו: אֶת-הָאֱלֹהִים, הִתְהַלֶּךְ-נֹחַ

⁹*These are the generations of Noah. Noah was a righteous man, blameless in his generation; Noah walked with God. (Gen. 6:9)*

The animals went into the ark in twos

ט שְׁנַיִם שְׁנַיִם בָּאוּ אֶל-נֹחַ, אֶל-הַתֵּבָה--זָכָר וּנְקֵבָה: כַּאֲשֶׁר צִוָּה אֱלֹהִים, אֶת-נֹחַ

⁹*two and two, male and female, went into the ark with Noah, as God had commanded Noah. (Gen. 7:9)*

When the sun passed into Aries, the land was dry. The lamb symbolizes land.

וַיְהִי בְּאַחַת וְשֵׁשׁ-מֵאוֹת שָׁנָה, בָּרִאשׁוֹן בְּאֶחָד לַחֹדֶשׁ, חָרְבוּ הַמַּיִם, מֵעַל הָאָרֶץ; וַיָּסַר
נֹחַ, אֶת-מִכְסֵה הַתֵּבָה, וַיַּרְא, וְהִנֵּה חָרְבוּ פְּנֵי הָאֲדָמָה. יד וּבַחֹדֶשׁ, הַשֵּׁנִי, בְּשִׁבְעָה
וְעֶשְׂרִים יוֹם, לַחֹדֶשׁ--יָבְשָׁה, הָאָרֶץ.

¹⁴In the second month, on the twenty-seventh day of the month, the earth was dry. (Gen. 8:13-14)

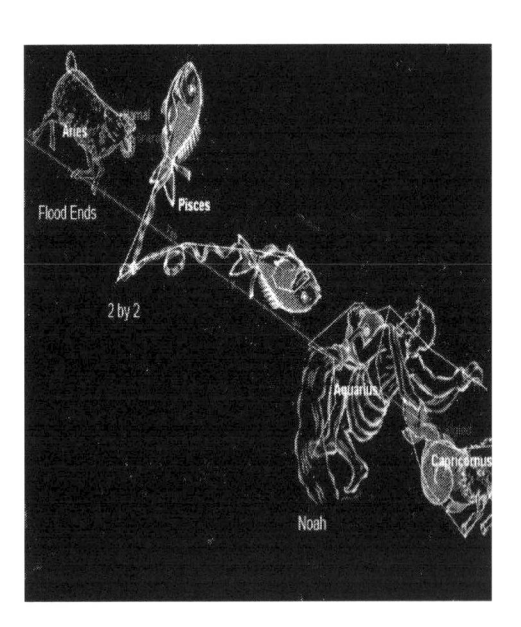

Second Image

The Argo Navis is such a large constellation that it was broken up into three constellations. Carina, Puppis and Vela, represent--respectively--the keel, stern and sail of a boat. Argo Navis lies far to the south on the celestial Tropic of Capricorn. The three sectors of Capricorn, Aquarius and Pisces contain a lot of watery constellations and were known to ancients as the Sea.

Noah sent a raven to seek dry land. The raven went to and fro until the waters dried up.

ז וַיְשַׁלַּח, אֶת-הָעֹרֵב; וַיֵּצֵא יָצוֹא וָשׁוֹב, עַד-יְבֹשֶׁת הַמַּיִם מֵעַל הָאָרֶץ.

⁷*and sent forth a raven; and it went to and fro until the waters were dried up from the earth. (Gen. 8:7)*

Then he sent a dove.

ח וַיְשַׁלַּח אֶת-הַיּוֹנָה, מֵאִתּוֹ--לִרְאוֹת הֲקַלּוּ הַמַּיִם, מֵעַל פְּנֵי הָאֲדָמָה.

⁸*Then he sent forth a dove from him, to see if the waters had subsided from the face of the ground; (Gen. 8:8)*

There is a classic Greek myth built around the Argo Navis, called Jason and the *Quest for the Golden Fleece*. The story follows the sun around the Zodiac.

Third Image

Noah got drunk and lay naked in his tent. Ham saw his nakedness and told his two brothers.

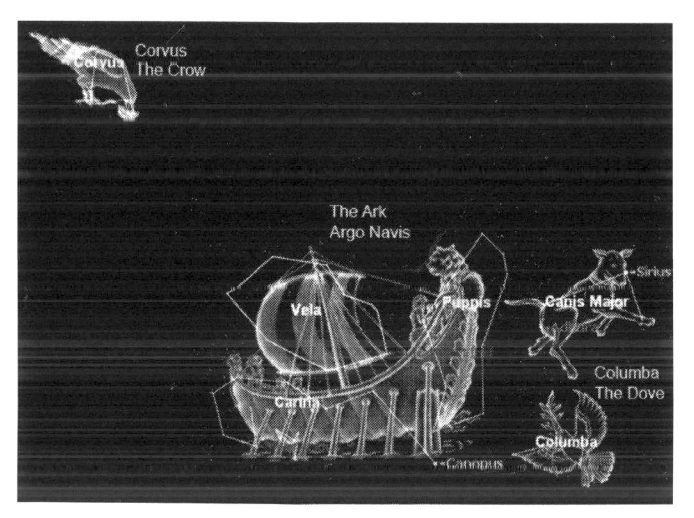

כ וַיָּחֶל נֹחַ, אִישׁ הָאֲדָמָה; וַיִּטַּע, כָּרֶם. כא וַיֵּשְׁתְּ מִן-הַיַּיִן, וַיִּשְׁכָּר; וַיִּתְגַּל, בְּתוֹךְ אָהֳלֹה. כב וַיַּרְא, חָם אֲבִי כְנַעַן, אֵת, עֶרְוַת אָבִיו; וַיַּגֵּד לִשְׁנֵי-אֶחָיו, בַּחוּץ.

[20] Noah was the first tiller of the soil. He planted a vineyard; [21] and he drank of the wine, and became drunk, and lay uncovered in his tent. [22] And Ham, the father of Canaan, saw the nakedness of his father, and told his two brothers outside. (Gen. 9:20-22)

In Taurus, we see Orion as Noah, Auriga as Ham and the Gemini twins as Shem and Jepheth. The three sons are looking down at their father. Shem and Japheth covered their father but did not see his nakedness.

כג וַיִּקַּח שֵׁם וָיֶפֶת אֶת-הַשִּׂמְלָה, וַיָּשִׂימוּ עַל-שְׁכֶם שְׁנֵיהֶם, וַיֵּלְכוּ אֲחֹרַנִּית, וַיְכַסּוּ אֵת עֶרְוַת אֲבִיהֶם; וּפְנֵיהֶם, אֲחֹרַנִּית, וְעֶרְוַת אֲבִיהֶם, לֹא רָאוּ.

[23] Then Shem and Japheth took a garment, laid it upon both their shoulders, and walked backward and covered the nakedness of their father; their faces were turned away, and they did not see their father's nakedness. (Gen. 9:23)

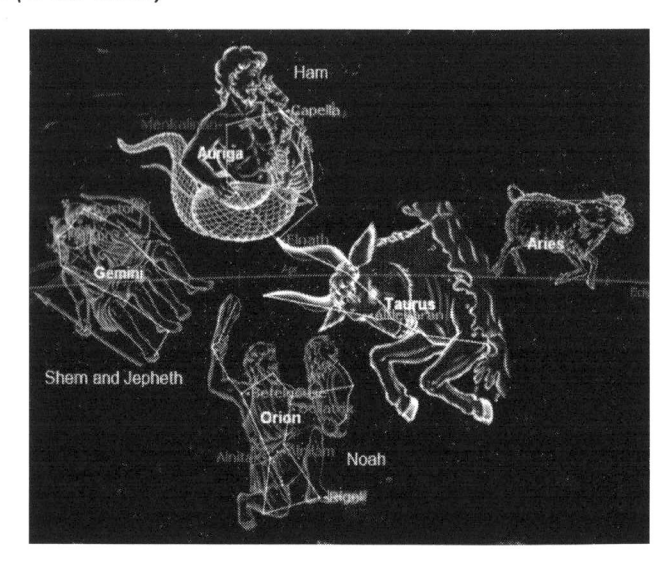

Epilogue

Shalom to All,

"The story of Noah encapsulates some of the most profound truths within the Torah. This one story captures the essence of Torah observance, the spiritual and physical void created in the absence of Torah observance, as well as the ultimate rectification (Teshuvah - Repentance) of the physical and metaphysical imbalance of the world we live in, created by our sins and yet remedied by Torah observance.

The story of Noah opens up with a piercing look into the actions of man and its correlation to the physical as well as metaphysical state of the earth. In describing the wickedness of man and its subsequent correspondence in the very estate of the earth, the Torah says: "Now the Earth had become CORRUPT before G-d; and the earth had become filled with violence. And G-d saw the Earth and behold it was corrupted, for all flesh had corrupted its way upon the earth" Genesis: 6:11-12. In the above verse, the Torah offers a direct correlation between actions of man and the estate of the earth. The idea that man and the earth coexist interdependently is not unique to the Torah alone. In fact, Science views the earth as a "Sentient Living Organism", which inhales, exhales, and responds to outside stimuli, I.e., Every single living organism. This concept of the earth's relativity to the actions of living organisms, namely Man, is known in Science as the "Gaia Hypothesis". This scientific idea, posits that our actions stimulate the earth both physically and metaphysically to act, or respond. The center of the Earth's core is the nucleus of the earth's intrinsic power. Earth's core contains an enormous mass of iron which spins at an enormous rate, while convulsed in fire. This creates an electromagnetic field which protects the earth's atmosphere. Earth essentially then has its own "SHIELD". Once this Shield is compromised or exposed, the entire system is threatened.

The nucleus of man's being is his soul (mind). Once the soul is compromised or exposed, his very life is threatened. Looking back now at the story of Noah, the Torah says that "the wickedness of man was Great upon the earth and his every "thought" was perpetually evil" Genesis:6:5. It then goes on to say that the "earth has become corrupt (as a result of man's deeds) before G-d; and the earth had become filled with violence" Genesis:6:11. Now, let's examine the language of the text. The Hebrew word for corrupt, as used in the above verse is V'TShaketותשחת or H'Shkitהשחית, which comes from the Hebraic root Shakatשחת, which means to self-destroy or self-mutilate. So, essentially the Torah is teaching us what science is only now beginning to confirm; that the Earth as a Sentient Living Organism, responds to the very thoughts and actions of man. Our thoughts and actions have a direct effect on the earth. Our negative actions can cause the earth to self-destruct, which at one time was considered at most, a brave "religious idea", is now being confirmed in modern science (Gaia Hypothesis). This is why the Torah emphasizes that only after viewing the wickedness of man, that G-d says behold the earth has become "corrupt" before Him, because not only was every living being behaving outside of the natural laws of the world (Torah), but our actions produced a metaphysical "ripple", which the very earth began to respond to negatively.

In the book of Proverbs, King Solomon says that the Torah תורה is a SHIELD מגן to us (Proverbs:2:7); once that shield is removed or exposed, we are open to destructive forces, both physical and metaphysical. Hence, just as we read above, as the Earth's core has a built-in Shield, so does man. Our shield is represented as our obedience to the Law and Order (Torah) of the Creator, who is the Author of All life. Which is why, in viewing the destructive nature of man's ways, G-d considers Noah, as the model for man's and the earth's redemption. The Torah says that Noah was a Righteous man, perfect in his generation, who thus found grace (mercy) in G-d's eyes (Genesis:6:8-9). Noah was commanded by G-d to build an Ark and to enter it with his entire family and to reach out to and bring everyone into the ark, which would willingly choose to enter, of both man and beast. There is so much depth of thought in the language used here. The word for ark in Hebrew is Teivahתבה, which also means word in Hebrew. Another closely related root is T'bonahתבונה, which both means to build and understanding. Thus, Noah's story teaches us something about spiritual redemption. When we enter the word (Ark) and immerse ourselves in it (Torah) we essentially are building a metaphysical edifice of truth, which will Shield us and all who we cause to join us. It will empower us to float in the depths of thought and redeem control and mastery of our very spirit or core.

Noah was told to build this ark with a window for illumination צהר (Genesis:6:16). This conveys the notion that the idea of pursuing wisdom should not be exclusive to you alone. Once we immerse ourselves in truth, it is our duty to "Illuminate" others with this truth as well, for our light is only as bright as the flame which sparked it. Noah was also told to build 3 decks or levels into this "ark". These 3 levels or decksallude to the 3 levels of our soul as mentioned in the Torah (neshama, ruach, &nefesh). Each species of animals sent to one of their levels, allude to the threefold stages of conquering the animal-soul within us, as represented by the above three names of our souls as mentioned in the Torah. The physical structure of the Ark had 3 dimensions, 300 cubits was its length, 50 cubits was its width, and 30 cubits was its height. In Hebrew, 300 is the numerical equivalent of the Hebrew letter Shin ש, 50 is the numerical equivalent of the Hebrew letter Nun נ, and 30 is the numerical equivalent of the Hebrew letter Lamed ל. These three letters spell the Hebrew word L'ashonלשון,

meaning tongue, speech, or language. What is language? Language is the verbal articulation of thought. The Torah says with regard to Noah's generation: "their every THOUGHT is evil" Genesis:6:5.

Thought is the "author" of all actions, first the mind thinks, the mouth speaks, and then the body acts. The 3 levels of our soul, the 3 levels or decks of the ark, the 3 dimensions of the ark (300, 50, 30), and the three ways our soul's desires become manifest (thought, speech, and action), all allude to the idea that the spoken word (speech) can manifest good or evil, as a tangible reality. The Torah teaches that the greatest form of repentance is via prayer (speech), hence the Jerusalem Temple contained within the "Holy of Holies", an altar of pure gold where not animals, but PRAYER (SPEECH) was offered. The power of speech in its positive state can literally work wonders. The book of Psalms records that G-d created the Universe with Speech (Psalms:33:9). The Hebrew noun for word is davar דבר, which also means "thing". Our thoughts reveal themselves in our speech, where it is then creative and a "thing" or substance is produced. The redemption of ourselves and the world at large is an insidious process, the more we immerse ourselves in the Ark of G-d's word (Torah) and draw others to see and benefit from its light, the more we produce a procreative effect, which will not only elevate us above the "flood" of the world's negative thoughts and actions, but it will also cause us to draw closer to the very source of our being, via repentance and prayer and thereby bind our very essence to His unchanging immutable will."

Written by: Avdiel Ben Levi

Aka Zion Lexx on Facebook

Special thanks to...

First and foremost I'd like to give all praises to The Most High King, The GOD of Abraham who has given me the intelligence to be able to write this book. I'd also like to thank the Hebrew War Machine #HWM!!! My fellow member of Shomrey HaTorah; Gabriel, thanks for the editing and great insight added to the book and also to SarYahnaiYah for his inspiration and loyalty. I'd also like to thank The Scorpion, Zion Lexx for bringing in-depth knowledge and for helping to producebooks for our generation. I want to thank my lovely wives, Rofaynuyah and Atarah who worked hard to edit this book along with the lil One Shanae Sheppard. To my elders, my father Chief Prince Tsippor, Crown Prince Zurishaddai, Chief of Chief Naphtali, Seren Ya'akov, Professor Rudolph Windsor, and an elder who truly supports me Elder Yosef.

References

The Babylonian Story of the Deluge as told by the Assyrian Tablets from Nineveh, by E.A Wallis Budge

Article 1993 entitled "New Theory is that a Lack of Oxygen Killed the Dinosaurs"- International Falls, Minnesota News

Jon Lieff, M.D. Entitled Meditation and Brain Changes: Recent Research and Applications.

Article entitled Endocrine Secretions during Sun Bathing by Wayne Purdin

Made in the USA
Columbia, SC
16 May 2025